# Contents

The publisher would like to thank Rawlings for their photographic contribution to this book. Front cover photograph courtesy of MLB Photos. Photographs on back cover, inside front cover, inside back cover and pages 3, 4, 11, 22, 36, 37, 39 and 40 courtesy of Baseball/Softball UK. All other photographs courtesy of Allsport UK Ltd. Illustrations by Dave Saunders.

*Note* Throughout the book players and officials are referred to individually as 'he'. This should, of course, be taken to mean 'he or she' where appropriate.

# Foreword

The sports of baseball and softball are governed in this country by the British Baseball Federation and the British Softball Federation respectively – jointly managed by Baseball/Softball UK.

Baseball is played in more than 106 countries all around the world. There are professional baseball leagues in over 10 countries throughout the Americas, Asia and Australia, but the 'pinnacle' of the game is Major League Baseball in North America, where all the best players in the world aspire to play.

Both baseball and fastpitch softball are full Olympic sports, and the international bodies – the International Association of Baseball Federations, and the International Softball Federation – also operate continental and world championships.

Baseball and softball provide excellent sporting opportunities for the whole population – male and female, whatever their age and level of ability. Both organisations run youth, recreational and competitive leagues, as well as elite-level programmes for national teams.

This book is intended as a clear and accessible introduction to baseball and softball, containing information on the basic rules, tactics and skills required to play both games. Also included is information on development programmes for schools and local communities, as well as useful contact addresses. Hopefully, it will motivate you to take up one or both of these exciting and rewarding sports.

Ian Smyth
Baseball/Softball UK

2

# Baseball

## Fundamentals of the game

The game of baseball is played between two teams of nine players who take it in turn to bat and field. A pitcher delivers the ball to a batter, who attempts to hit it and run around as many of the bases on the baseball 'diamond' as possible before the ball is retrieved and returned under control by the fielding (defensive) team.

The object is to score more 'runs' than the opposition, and a run is scored when a player on the batting (offensive) side advances around all three 'bases' and back to 'home plate'. A run can be scored in stages, in that the batter does not have to get all the way around on one hit. If he does, this is called a 'home run'.

The aim of the defensive team is to prevent the batting side from scoring runs and to get the batters out (*see* p. 13). Once three players on the offensive team are out, the two teams switch: the defensive team comes in to bat and the batting team goes out on to the field to defend. An inning is complete once both teams have batted – the first team batting at the 'top' of the inning and the second at the 'bottom' – and the game is over once nine innings have been played. If after nine innings the scores are level, the game continues until one team wins.

However, the essence of the game of baseball is the duel between pitcher and batter. The pitcher has to outwit the batter using different pitches, speeds and positions in the strike zone, while the batter's job is to get on base safely, and then attempt to score a run.

# The playing area

The baseball field is illustrated in Figure 1. It is formed by two 'foul' lines that run at right angles to each other from home plate through first and third bases creating an arc. The inner part of this segment is called the infield; the outer part is called the outfield.

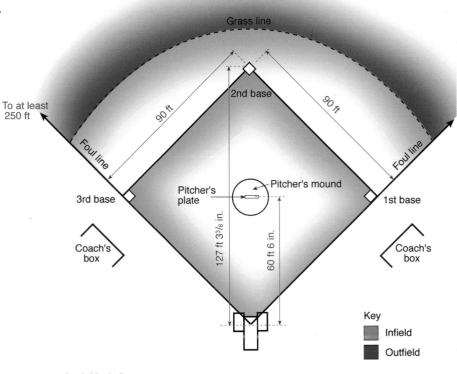

▲ Fig. 1   The field of play

# The infield (diamond)

The infield is formed by a diamond with a base at each corner. Each of these bases must be touched by the runner to score a run. Within the infield there are the following important areas.

## Batter's boxes

Either side of home plate is a batter's box, where the batter must stand when hitting the ball (*see* fig. 2, p. 6). If the batter hits the ball while out of this box, he will be called out.

## First, second and third bases

Members of the batting side run from the batter's box and move in an anti-clockwise direction around the infield diamond. At each corner of the diamond (first, second and third) a base is secured to the ground. This is a white canvas bag, 15 in. (38 cm) square and filled with foam. The distance between bases is 90 ft (27.4 m); this has remained constant throughout the history of the game.

## Home plate

The home plate is the fourth and final base. It is a five-sided piece of white rubber measuring 17 in. (43.2 cm) in width and 23 in. (58.4 cm) from front to rear, with the sharp point facing the catcher. It is secured flush to the ground and bordered by a strip of black.

## Fair territory

This is the part of the playing field within the lines drawn from home plate through first and third bases.

## Pitcher's plate

The pitcher delivers the ball to the batter from a raised mound in the centre of the diamond – the 'pitcher's mound' – located 60 ft 6 in. (18.5 m) away from the batter. The mound has a radius of 18 ft (5.5 m).

On top of the mound is a rectangular piece of whitened rubber – the 'pitcher's plate' (also called a 'pitching rubber'). The plate measures 24 x 6 in. (60.4 x 15.2 cm), and must be no more than 10 in. (25.4 cm) above the level of home plate. The pitcher must be in contact with this when he starts his delivery.

## Catcher's box

Behind home plate is the catcher's box – 43 in. (109.2 cm) wide – within which the catcher fields the ball. The catcher must stay in this box until the pitcher has delivered the ball (*see* fig. 2, p. 6).

# The outfield

The lines defining fair territory (*see* above) continue through first and third bases for a distance of at least 250 ft (76 m) to the outfield fence, with flags situated at the extreme ends (*see* fig. 1, p. 4). These lines are called 'foul lines', because any ball which falls outside them is deemed to be in 'foul territory' and therefore 'foul'. The outfield is the area within the two foul lines but behind the infield.

# Non-playing areas

## Bench ('dug-out')

While not active, team members, coaches and managers sit in separate bench areas, usually situated between home plate and first base, and home plate and third base.

## Bull pen

This is an area set aside for relief pitchers (*see* p. 10) to warm up and practise throwing.

## On-deck circles

A batter waiting to take his turn at bat practises his swings in the 'on-deck circles', situated in foul territory.

## Dead ball area

This extends in straight lines from the backstop net, which should be 60 ft (18 m) behind the home plate, to the left and right outfield or foul territory.

(Most baseball fields will have some form of backstop to prevent the ball from flying straight back behind the batter and into the crowd.)

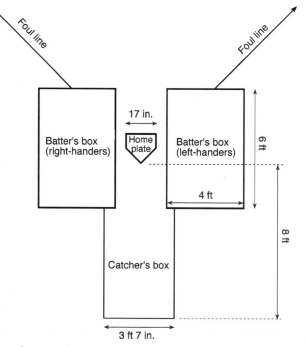

▲ *Fig. 2 Home plate area*

# Equipment

The two main pieces of equipment are the bat and the ball. Other equipment, including gloves, protective equipment and field equipment, is necessary for an organised game.

## The ball

The ball is made from white leather bound around a core of cork. It is spherical, has a circumference of between 9 and 9¼ in. (22.6–23.5 cm), and weighs between 5 and 5¼ oz (142–9 g). The ball is stitched together forming raised seams, which are used by the pitcher to make the ball curve in the air during delivery to the batter.

## The bat

This is a smooth, rounded stick with a maximum diameter of 2¾ in. (7 cm), and a maximum length of 42 in. (106.7 cm). (Smaller bats are available for young players.)

Most players use bats that weigh between 28 and 34 oz (794–964 g) – although Babe Ruth used a bat that weighed 54 oz (1531 g). Beginners often try to use the biggest bat available, under the mistaken impression that it will enable them to hit the ball harder and further. However, a light bat is easier to control, and therefore makes it easier to hit the ball.

Most amateurs will use aluminium bats due to their superior durability; these will last much longer than wooden bats, and so will be less expensive in the long run. In the major leagues in America, however, professionals are only allowed to use wooden bats, generally made of ash.

# Clothing

The usual clothing consists of a base-ball cap, shirt, baseball pants, belt, socks and shoes. These are in team colours; the team's name is often displayed on the front of the shirt, while the player's name and number is on the back. Cleated shoes are permitted except in junior baseball, but the soles vary depending on the playing surface.

# Protective equipment

## Gloves

All fielders, including the pitcher, wear lightweight leather gloves while they are fielding. These have a pocket ('webbing') which allows the player to catch the ball more easily, and are worn on the weaker hand – the left if you are right-handed, leaving your stronger, right hand free to throw the ball. Generally, infielders' gloves are smaller than those of the outfielders, to enable a quick transfer of the ball from the glove to the throwing hand. Plays in the infield have to be executed quickly; the size of the infielders' gloves helps to facilitate this.

The catcher wears a specialised 'catcher's mitt' which is highly padded for protection: during the course of a game he will receive the ball more than 150 times, at speeds of over 90 miles (145 km) per hour in the professional game. The first baseman also has a specialised glove, which is a little bigger than a standard fielder's glove.

## Helmets

In baseball it is now mandatory for all batters to wear batting helmets. These are plastic with foam padding, and protect the player from potential head injuries caused by a thrown or batted ball while either batting or baserunning.

## The catcher

Due to the nature of his playing position (*see* p. 10), the catcher needs to be especially well protected. As well as his mitt (see above), he wears a helmet, a face mask, a throat protector, a chest protector, a cup and leg guards – equipment that is often referred to collectively as the 'tools of ignorance'. Modern catching equipment is lightweight and user-friendly. It provides adequate protection while allowing the catcher freedom of movement.

# Playing positions

## The pitcher

The pitcher's role is the most important on any baseball team, with a good pitcher nearly always holding the advantage over a good batter. Once he has pitched, he becomes another infielder, ready to catch or stop batted balls and throw to bases as required

The pitcher needs to be able to throw the ball both fast and accurately, as well as to make it move in the air (*see* pp. 18–20). This requires a great deal of skill. During a baseball game the pitcher will probably throw between 80 and 120 pitches – very demanding physically, and often why the 'starting' pitcher will be replaced by one or more 'relief' pitchers in the course of the game.

## The catcher

The catcher is involved in every play,

and in most cases advises the pitcher on which pitches to throw.

From his position within the catcher's box behind home plate (*see* fig. 2, p. 6), the catcher can see the whole field of play and can thus, with the manager and base coaches, direct both the infield and outfield – essentially acting as a 'general'. His main task is to catch all pitches that pass beyond the batter, although he also guards home plate against incoming baserunners and tries to prevent them from scoring.

## First baseman

When the batter hits the ball, it is fielded and often thrown to first base. The first baseman catches the ball in his mitt and tries to get the batter/runner out by touching the base (usually with his foot) before the runner arrives. He also guards part of the right side of the

infield against 'fly' and 'ground' balls (*see* p. 14), so his catching skills are paramount; being tall, and also left-handed, is an advantage in receiving any errant throws.

## Middle infielders

The second baseman and shortstop make up the middle infield. As well as receiving catches made to second base, the second baseman also guards much of the right side of the infield, so should not remain on second unless a throw is coming in. The shortstop stands between second and third bases and tries to stop or catch any ball hit towards left field. He is also in a good position to make throws to any base.

## Third baseman

This player guards the area near third base and will usually take throws to third as well. He therefore needs good reflexes (since the ball is often hit hard in that direction) and a strong throwing arm, as his ability to field 'line drives' (*see* p. 14) and throws from the outfielders and relay them accurately to all bases can determine the outcome of a match.

# Outfielders (left, centre and right field)

The outfield positions are slightly more flexible than the infield, with the players being positioned differently for different batters. For example, if a big hitter is at bat, they might be moved back; if a left-handed batter is up, they might be shifted around towards right field. Outfielders tend to be very fast athletes able to chase down and catch 'fly balls' (*see* p. 14). Strength and accuracy are important elements in their throws to the infield.

# The batter

Players bat in a pre-arranged order or 'line-up', which goes in rotation (*see* p. 29). In other words, when the last batter in the order is on base or has been put out, the first batter comes up again. However, when batters are 'out', they are not out of either the game or the inning permanently. For example, if the first batter – or 'lead-off' man – is out, but the team is still at bat by the time his name comes up again in the batting order, he goes up to bat again. If the final out in an inning is made by the fifth batter, the sixth in line will be first up at bat in the next inning. The 'out' can therefore be seen as being against the team rather than the player.

The batter takes up his position in the batting box facing the pitcher and tries to hit the ball. If he does put the ball into play, he cannot elect to receive another pitch, but must advance to first base, where he becomes a 'baserunner' if he reaches it safely.

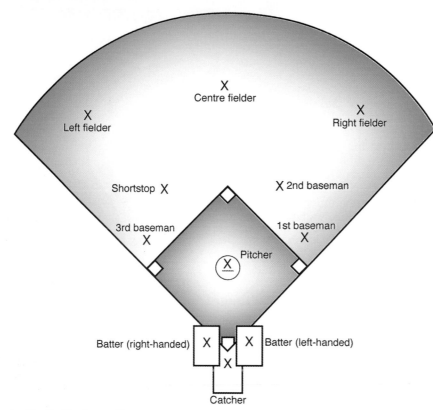

Centre fielder

Left fielder

Right fielder

Shortstop

2nd baseman

3rd baseman

1st baseman

Pitcher

Batter (right-handed)

Batter (left-handed)

Catcher

▲ *Fig. 3  Playing positions*

# The basic rules

## Balls and strikes

A pitched ball is described as either a 'strike' or a 'ball'. A strike is basically a good pitch and a ball, a bad one. Using an overarm or side-arm action, the pitcher attempts to throw a 'strike', whereby the ball passes through the 'strike zone'. (For a description of pitching techniques, *see* pp. 18–22, and batting technique, *see* p. 23.)

### The strike zone

This is an imaginary three-dimensional column of space with depth, width and corners corresponding to the shape of the home plate and positioned between the batter's knees and mid point of the chest (*see* fig. 4). A ball needs only touch (pass through) any part of this zone to be called a 'strike': outside of this space and the pitch is called a 'ball'. This is judged by the home-plate umpire (*see* p. 13), whose decision is final.

The batter is allowed three strikes at which he can attempt a hit. These are also called by the home-plate umpire if:

• the batter swings at but misses any pitch – even if it would have been a ball
• the batter hits a ball into foul territory (except on the third strike)
• the batter swings at a strike and the ball hits him
• a 'foul tip' occurs, where the ball flies off the bat and is caught by the catcher.

If he fails to hit the ball before three strikes are called, he is 'struck out' and retired. If, however, the pitcher pitches four balls – bad pitches which are outside the strike zone and which the batter makes no attempt to hit – the batter will walk to first base (*see* p. 14 and also 'intentional walks', p. 26).

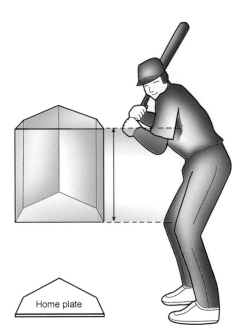

Home plate

▲  *Fig. 4   The strike zone*

# The count

This is the way in which the umpire keeps track of the number of balls and strikes on the batter after each pitch. Balls are listed first, so a batter with a count of 2–0 ('two-and-oh') has two balls and no strikes on him. A 'full count' is when there are three balls and two strikes: another ball, and the batter walks to first base; another strike, and the batter is 'struck out'.

---

**Types of hit**
*Fly ball* – a batted ball hit into the air
*Line drive* – a batted ball hit into the air, but hard and on a flat trajectory
*Ground ball* – a batted ball that bounces on the ground
*Bunt* (*see* p. 30) – a tactical hit where the ball rolls slowly on the infield

---

## Retiring a batter

Apart from being struck out, the other most common methods of retiring a batter are:

● *a catch*: if the batted ball is caught by a fielder before touching the ground

● *an illegally batted ball*: if the batter steps out of his box to hit the ball (on fair or foul hits)
● *impeding the catcher in any way*
● *run out on first*: if the first baseman touches his base with the ball in hand before the batter reaches it.

## Becoming a baserunner

A batter completes his time at bat when he is either put out, or becomes a baserunner. He becomes a runner when:

● he hits a ball into fair territory
● he misses the third strike, but it is not caught by the catcher either, provided that first base is unoccupied, or there are two outs
● he hits a home run
● a fair ball is deflected by a fielder into foul territory.

Once he has completed his time at bat, he must drop (never throw) the bat before proceeding to first base. A batter becomes a runner and is entitled to first base when:

● four balls have been called by the umpire: this is known as a 'walk' or a 'base on balls'
● he is touched by a pitched ball: this is intended to dissuade pitchers from throwing directly at batters – although the batter has to make an attempt to get out of the way of the pitch
● the pitcher 'balks' (*see* p. 22)
● a fielder interferes with him: any such interference usually comes from the catcher – i.e. the catcher's mitt makes contact with the bat during the batter's swing

## Baserunning

Once he has reached a base, a runner cannot return to the base he previously occupied if the pitcher is holding the ball, has taken up his position and is in contact with the pitcher's plate.

### Singles, doubles, triples and home runs

If a batter reaches first base safely, this is known as a 'single' base hit. If he reaches second or third bases safely, this is known as a 'double' or 'triple' respectively. If the batter advances all the way around the bases with one hit, this is called a 'home run'. If there are no other runners on base ahead of him, it is worth one run. If there are runners on all three bases when he hits the ball – i.e. the 'bases are loaded' – it is called a 'grand slam' and is worth four runs as each runner in front of him scores as well.

## Force plays

A base cannot be occupied by two runners. This means that a runner sometimes has to advance to the next base even if that baseman has the ball and can get him out by tagging either him or the base (see below). This is called a 'force play', and the runner is 'forced out' – something that can happen at any base, including home plate.

---

**Examples of force plays**
If a batter hits a ball into fair territory, he has to run to first base. Any runner already there is therefore forced to run on to second, and any runner on second is therefore forced

---

to run on to third etc., irrespective of whether or not they may be out. If, on the other hand, there are runners on first and third bases but second is vacant, only the runner on first is in a forced situation. There is no runner on second base forcing the runner on third to advance.

---

# Retiring runners

As a runner advances around the diamond, he must touch every base in turn. If he fails to do so, the fielding team can appeal, and the runner can be given out by the umpire.

A runner must not run more than 3 ft (0.91 m) away from a direct line between the bases to avoid being tagged out (see p. 17). He will also be called out if:

- he interferes intentionally with a thrown ball, or hinders a fielder making a play on a batted ball
- he is hit by a batted ball in fair territory
- he is tagged, when the ball is live, while off a base – or fails to reach the

next base before a fielder tags him (or the base, on a force play)
- he passes another runner, unless that one is out
- he does not 'tag up' when a fly ball is caught: a runner must be in contact with the base until after the ball is caught; only then can he attempt to run to the next base.

---

**Examples of 'tagging up'**
If there is a runner on third, and the batter hits a long fly ball to the outfield, the baserunner must 'tag up': he must stand on third base until the ball is caught. If he feels the ball has been hit far enough and he has time, he may attempt to run home (see p. 30). If not, he will stay at third.

If this same runner feels that the hit will not be caught, he can gamble and leave third base. However, if a fielder does make the catch, the baserunner must return to third – either tagging up and (if time) attempting to run to home plate again or staying on third base. In this case, if the defence throws the ball to third base before the runner returns, he will be called out.

---

# Defensive skills

## Fielding stance/ ready position

When fielding, the feet are positioned a little more than shoulder-width apart. Toes pointing straight ahead and body weight equally distributed on the balls of the feet, the fielder bends at the hips, leaning forwards with his head up and back parallel to the ground. The hands are held palms up and fingers down, in front of the body between spread knees.

## Catching

Whenever possible, the fielder should catch a thrown or batted ball with two hands. The glove's webbing between thumb and index finger should be used to pick it out of the air, before the fingers close around the ball and the ungloved hand covers it as well to prevent it from dropping out again. By

covering the ball like this, the fielder also ensures that his throwing hand is in the right position to pick the ball out of the glove quickly in readiness to throw. The fingers point downwards for a catch below the belt.

If the ball is running along the ground, the glove should be held at ground level, as it is easier to follow a ball upwards than downwards.

## Throwing

The over-arm throw is the fastest and most accurate throw to use. The side-arm throw, commonly used by infielders, is slower and has a tendency to curve.

All throws use the following action: the player looks at the target, steps directly towards it, cocks his arm (the elbow should be higher than the shoulder with wrist flexed backwards for the over-arm throw), throws and follows through by bending for-

wards and bringing the arm across the body.

The use of a short 'crow hop' helps when executing a long throw: the fielder steps with the leading foot, hops on to the rear foot and steps again with the leading foot to gain extra momentum.

16

# Tagging out

A fielder can 'tag' out a runner out who is not on base by touching him with the ball. The exceptions are:

- *on first base* – where the runner does not have to stop dead on first base but can make contact with it and run beyond in a straight line (to ensure that speed and momentum are not lost when sprinting towards it from home

plate). He can then walk back to it safely without being tagged out. If, on the other hand, the runner passes first base and turns into the field of play with the intention of running on towards second base, he can be tagged out
- *on a forced play* (*see* p. 16) – where either runner or the base to which he must advance can be tagged.

# Pitching techniques

The game of baseball revolves around the confrontation between the pitcher and batter. It is the pitcher's task to prevent the batter from making a base hit, and this is achieved by a combination of:

- speed – which can exceed 90 mph (145 kph) in top competition
- trajectory – how the ball moves through the air: the pitcher can grip the ball in different ways so that the seams catch the air and put spin on the ball to make it curve and dip (*see* pp. 19–22)
- and placement – where the ball

touches or crosses through the strike zone.

The type of delivery used depends on the player at bat, the game's score, how many runners are on base and how many 'outs' have been gained. The pitcher takes advice by means of signals from the catcher.

## Starting positions

There are two legal pitching positions – the 'wind-up' and 'set' positions.

### The wind-up position
The pitcher will generally pitch from the wind-up position when there are no runners on base. He must stand facing the batter, with his back, or 'pivot' foot on the pitcher's plate. In making his delivery he can take one step backwards and one step forwards with his non-pivot foot.

From the wind-up position the pitcher may:

- deliver the ball to the batter
- 'disengage' the rubber by stepping off it with his pivot foot.

**The set position**

The pitcher generally pitches from the set position when there are runners on base. The position is indicated by him when he stands facing the batter, with his entire pivot foot on – or in front of and in contact with – the pitcher's plate. The ball is held in both hands in front of his body, and the pitcher comes to a complete stop.

From the set position the pitcher may:

- deliver the ball to the batter
- throw to a base
- step backwards off the pitcher's plate with his pivot foot.

After the pitcher assumes either the wind-up or the set position, any natural movement associated with his delivery of the ball to the batter commits him to the pitch.

# Types of pitch

## Fastball

Practically all pitchers will have a fastball in their armoury, and by beating the batter's reflexes to gain a strike, hard-throwing pitchers use these to intimidate batters. There are two main types:

- four-seam fastball – this pitch will give the ball a true line to the catcher with little or no deviation
- two-seam fastball – due to wind resistance against the seams, this pitch should deviate a little more than a four-seam fastball, dropping or sinking more and hopefully fooling the batter.

The intention of the fastball is to beat the batter with pure pace. However, even the fastest pitchers will get hit if they are unable to throw another type of pitch. Therefore, to be effective it is vital to have at least one more variety in their repertoire, making it difficult for the batter to anticipate what is coming next.

## Curveball

As its name suggests, this pitch curves through the air, beating the batter with movement rather than speed. When the ball is released, the pitcher snaps his wrist, imparting spin on the ball to make it break downwards and sideways. A right-handed pitcher will make the ball break from right to left; a left-hander will move the ball from left to right. Figure 5 shows the path of the curveball for a right-handed pitcher.

## Slider

This is essentially a cross between a curveball and a fastball. The slider will break less than a curveball and later in its flight. Batters think that it is a fastball, and are deceived by the last-minute break of the ball over home plate.

## Change-up

This pitch aims to deceive the batter in its slower speed to the plate. The pitcher attempts to make the delivery look exactly the same as for a fastball, hopefully forcing the batter to mistime his swing.

## Forkball or split-fingered fastball

As the name suggests, this pitch is a variation on the fastball. Unlike the fastball, however, the fingers are spread wide, the ball resting between the index and second fingers. The delivery is the same as for a fastball, with the ball travelling directly towards the plate before it breaks sharply downwards just beforehand.

## Screwball

The screwball is essentially the curveball in reverse.

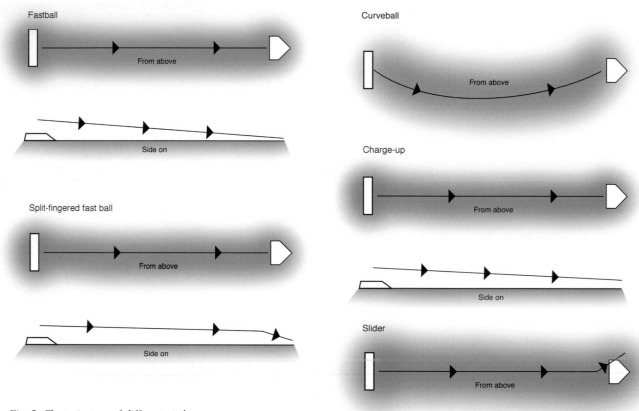

▲ *Fig. 5  The trajectory of different pitches*

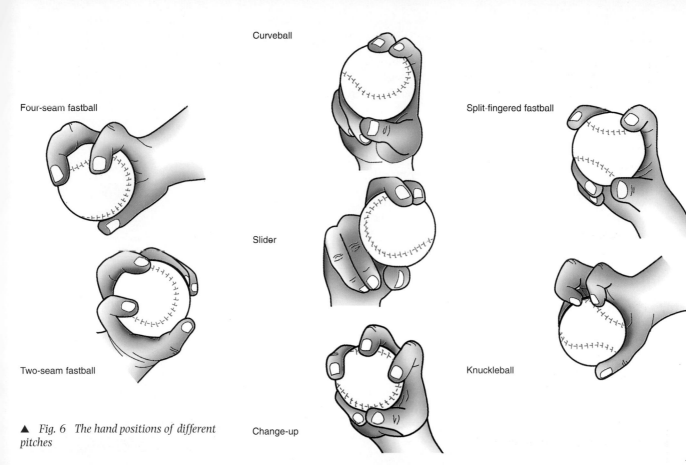

Four-seam fastball

Two-seam fastball

Curveball

Slider

Change-up

Split-fingered fastball

Knuckleball

▲ *Fig. 6 The hand positions of different pitches*

## Knuckleball

The knuckleball is held between the thumb and knuckles. Due to this grip, the ball will not spin in flight, but it will move, due to air resistance on the seams.

This pitch works best in hot, humid conditions. The movement of the ball is unpredictable – not even the pitcher and catcher know what the ball will do. If the knuckleball is thrown too hard, it will flatten out, fail to move in the air, and be easy to hit. It's a diffi-cult pitch to master, but can be extremely effective.

## Illegal pitches

### Altering the condition of the ball

The pitcher is not allowed to alter the condition or nature of the ball. He may rub it with his bare hands, but cannot rub it on his clothing or use any substance to alter it in any way – e.g. using saliva to change its flight through the air in the so-called 'spit ball'. The penalty for violation of this rule is that the umpire calls a ball and gives the pitcher a warning. If the pitcher re-offends in the same game, he is ejected.

### Throwing at the batter

The pitcher is not allowed to throw at the batter intentionally. Obviously this is very dangerous, and can be used as a means of intimidation. If, in the umpire's opinion, such a violation occurs, he may eject the pitcher from the game, or officially warn either the pitcher and manager or both teams.

### Balks

This is an illegal movement by the pitcher aimed at intentionally deceiving the offensive team with a runner or runners on base. The penalty is that the ball is dead, and all runners advance one base. If there is a runner on third base, he advances to home plate and scores a run.

# Offensive skills

## Batting

It has been said that the single most difficult skill in sport is to hit a base-ball. The combination of a round bat, round ball, and pitches of different speeds, trajectories and locations means that even batters in the major leagues will only hit the ball safely on three out of every ten attempts.

The stance of the batter, and the way in which he grips the bat, are fundamental to the success of his swing. The types of grip are illustrated in Figure 7.

A right-handed batter stands in the batting box, left side on to the pitcher, gripping the bat in both hands, with his weight on his back (right) foot. He watches the pitcher, trying to see the ball at its release point, but only has a fraction of a second to decide whether to swing at the pitch or leave it.

The batter keeps his eye on the ball all the way to the point of contact with the bat. He begins the swing by shifting his weight on to his front (left) foot, twisting the body to open up his hips, then shoulders, which pull the bat through to meet the ball and onwards into the follow-through. The bat must make good contact and connect with the ball at the correct moment to put it into play: too early or too late and it will travel into foul territory.

Standard grip

Choking up on the bat, to allow better control

▲  *Fig. 7  Batting grips*

# Baserunning

There is a great deal of skill and judgement involved in baserunning and a good runner can often gain an advantage by forcing the defensive team to panic and make mistakes.

A baserunner is essentially a sprinter, and speed between bases is important. However, while sprinting he must also be aware of the state of the game and react accordingly. He should consider the number of outs, which bases are occupied, if the pitcher is going to attempt to throw to his base, or if a baseman is going to tag him off base.

To obtain this kind of information, he looks for signals from the coaches, who stand in their marked boxes at first and third bases in foul territory (*see* p. 32). For example, the base coaches decide if a runner should try to 'steal' to the next base (*see* p. 30), or continue running past third for home plate and a potential run.

# Sliding

Sliding the last few feet into base along the ground is important because:

- it helps evade the tag: the runner presents a smaller, and therefore more difficult target for the fielder to tag
- it allows the runner to maintain his running speed until the last second
- the action of the runner's foot hitting the bag slows his momentum, and can enable him to regain his feet ready to advance to the next base if appropriate.

In other words, it increases the chances that the runner will reach the base safely.

However, a runner may overslide the base because of his speed, and then be in danger of being tagged out while not in contact with it. Sliding can also be dangerous, so players must be coached in the correct methods. It is an evasive manoeuvre and should never be used to injure an opponent. Once a runner has decided to slide, he must never change his mind as hesitancy may cause injury.

All slides are basically executed in the same way, and there are three main types.

## Bent-leg slide

Probably the most commonly used slide in the game, the runner bends his take-off foot underneath his body and slides on it. The lead foot contacts the base and, if a bad throw has been made, a quick recovery puts the runner in a position to advance to the next base.

## Hook slide

This is a more extreme slide, the main purpose being to evade tagging. As he approaches the base, the runner stretches out his lead foot to hook the base, while the take-off foot kicks up and away from it. The arms are thrown back over the head and the whole body is flat to the ground.

## Head-first slide

Not as dangerous as it might seem, the runner leans forwards so as to get as close to the ground as possible before diving head first. He takes off with one foot and slides on his chest, arms out, head up and eyes looking towards the base.

# Strategy

## Signals

Both the offensive and defensive teams use signs and signals, which are responsible for most tactical moves made during the game. Each team manager tries to outwit his opposite number, while coaches on the field give out many false signals to confuse the opposition.

It is important that signals are worked out and memorised beforehand for aspects like:

- the type of pitch
- the 'pitch out' (*see* p. 26)
- the 'intentional walk' (*see* p. 26)
- instructing the batter not to hit or swing at the pitch
- the bunt (*see* p. 30)
- instructing a runner to steal a base (see p. 30)
- the hit and run (*see* p. 31)
- cancelling the intended set play.

## Defensive tactics

The overall objective of all defensive strategy is to prevent the opposition from scoring runs. This is done primarily by preventing the advancement of runners into scoring positions – anywhere from second base onwards. With this in mind, all fielders should follow these general guidelines:

- always keep the ball in front of you
- if you cannot catch the ball, knock it down and stop it
- throw ahead of the runner
- make accurate throws.

Each team member also needs to know his responsibilities in any given set play or game situation, as well as being able to 'read the game' and know the team's overall defensive strategy. For example, to prevent a baserunner from stealing a base, the pitcher keeps the runner uncertain of his intentions and the catcher throws the ball rapidly to the bases.

Within this framework, there are specific defences to combat specific situations.

## Pitch-out

This is when the pitcher deliberately throws a pitch that is *outside* the strike zone. This is so that the catcher can try to throw out a runner who is attempting, or is likely, to steal a base. The signal is given and the pitch comes in wide to the awaiting catcher, who then throws to second or third base for the possible tag.

## Intentional walk

Pitchers usually attempt to throw strikes in order to retire the batter. If the pitcher *intentionally* throws four balls, the batter advances to first base on an 'intentional walk'. This is used to:

• by-pass a strong hitter
• bring a weak hitter up to bat – e.g. when there are two outs.

## Infield fly

If the batter hits a fly ball to the infield with runners on first and second bases, or with bases loaded, and if there are fewer than two outs, the umpire will call an 'infield fly'. In this instance the batter is automatically out if the ball is fair: the defence do not even have to catch the ball. This is done to prevent the defence from deliberately allowing the ball to fall to the ground and creating a force play (e.g. to attempt a double or triple play – *see* p. 29).

## Pop fly coverage

A pop-up fly is a ball that is hit high into the air by the batter, which is then caught. The defence requires the whole team to understand the following rules:

• players aiming to catch a fly ball must call loudly, 'I've got it!'
• centre field has priority over all other fielders
• all outfielders have priority over all infielders

• infielders have priority over the catcher
• first and third basemen should make all catches near the mound, in front of home plate, down the sidelines and near the dug-outs
• shortstop and second baseman should catch all balls down the left field and right field lines respectively, behind the bases
• catchers should catch pop-ups behind the plate that other infielders cannot handle
• unless absolutely necessary, the pitcher should not catch pop flies.

## Cut-offs and relays

Cut-offs and relays are defensive plays used when the ball is hit to the outfield with runners on base. The main purpose is to recover the ball from the outfield, under control and in the shortest time possible. If executed effectively, the fielding team may stop runners from taking an extra base – thus keeping them from reaching a scoring position whilst at the same time setting up double-play possibilities (*see* p. 29).

A 'cut-off' is a player who receives a throw from the outfield, thus linking the infield and outfield in order to shorten the length of throw back to the bases. His role is to act as a 'target man' for the outfielder, and purely by being in the correct position, the cut-off may prevent runners from trying to take an extra base.

The cut-off must receive the ball and quickly 'relay' it to the correct base. He will be told by the respective baseman where to throw the ball – or, in fact, if he should hold on to it and not make a throw.

**Example of a cut-off and relay**
When a runner is on first base and a batter hits a single to centre field, the shortstop is the cut-off. His aim is to prevent the runner from passing second base and advancing to third, and he does this by assuming a position about 40 ft (12.2 m) in front of third base (as viewed from the outfield). The centre fielder then throws to third base, aiming for the cut-off's head (*see* fig. 8).

If the throw is on target, the third baseman says nothing and the shortstop lets the ball go directly to third base. If the throw is on line but not strong enough, the third baseman shouts, 'Relay! Relay!', and the shortstop then cuts-off the ball and relays it to him.

If the runner is definitely going to make third, the third baseman shouts, 'Cut!' If the cut-off hears nothing else, he keeps the ball and runs back towards the infield. However, if the batter has reached first base and is trying to get to second, the shout will be, 'Cut 2!', and the cut-off will relay the ball to second base.

The cut-off is important here. If the outfielder throws a long, arcing ball to third base – missing the cut-off – it will take too long to get there. The runner will probably be safe at third base, and the batter will get into scoring position at second.

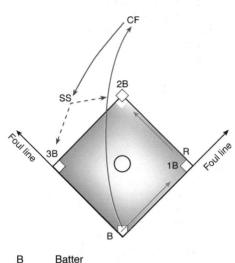

| B | Batter |
|---|---|
| R | Runner on 1st base |
| 1B | 1st baseman |
| 2B | 2nd baseman |
| 3B | 3rd baseman |
| CF | Centre field |
| SS | Shortstop |
| ⟶ | Single to centre field |
| ⟶ | Path of batter and runner |
| ⟶ | Throw to shortstop (cut-off) |
| - - ⟶ | Relay to 3rd base or cut-off to 2nd |

▲ *Fig. 8 Example of a cut-off and relay*

Fielders acting as cut-offs for various plays are as follows:

*For plays to home:*
- a hit to right field – first baseman
- a hit to centre field – first baseman
- a hit to left field – third baseman.

*For plays to third base:*
- a hit to right field – shortstop
- a hit to centre field – shortstop.

# Run down

This is is one of the most exciting plays to watch, bringing spectators to their feet. It occurs in an unforced situation when a runner is caught off-base – between two bases and trapped between two or more fielders with the ball – so that he cannot run to either base without risking a tag.

The play is simple, and with practice should always result in an out. Players involved in the run-down play must ensure that they move away from the play when they have thrown the ball, because if the runner is hindered the umpire will call 'interference' and the runner will be safe.

**Examples of run-downs**
If the runner is stationary, the fielder should run as fast as he can after the runner, holding the ball in a throwing position ready for the receiving fielder's call. The receiver closes in on the runner as far as he can and prepares to call for the throw. The ball is not thrown until the receiver calls 'Now!' He then catches the ball and tags the runner.

If the runner has sprinted towards the next base, the fielder with the ball throws to that baseman to head him off but must then hold his ground for the return throw. When the runner sees that the baseman ahead of him has the ball and can tag him out, he will double back on himself in an attempt to get back to base. The first fielder then calls for the return throw and tags the runner out.

## 'Double' and 'triple plays'

A 'double' or 'triple play' is when the fielding team manages to get two or three offensive players out in one go.

---

### Example of a double play

There is a runner on first base and the next batter hits a ground ball towards the shortstop. The batter must run to first base, and the runner on first is forced to run to second. The fielding team therefore has a choice of two runners to get out.

However, if there are less than two outs, they could try to go for both (see fig. 9). Typically, the shortstop throws the ball to the second baseman to retire the first runner, and the second baseman then immediately throws on to first base. If the throw reaches the first baseman before the batter reaches the base, he too will be out.

---

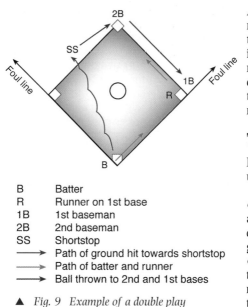

| | |
|---|---|
| B | Batter |
| R | Runner on 1st base |
| 1B | 1st baseman |
| 2B | 2nd baseman |
| SS | Shortstop |
| ⟶ | Path of ground hit towards shortstop |
| ⟶ | Path of batter and runner |
| ⟶ | Ball thrown to 2nd and 1st bases |

▲  *Fig. 9  Example of a double play*

## Offensive tactics

An essential part of baseball strategy revolves around team offence, with the batting team using various plays in order to advance runners and score runs. Aggressive offence can intimidate the opposition into making mistakes, which will eventually lead to runs being scored.

### The batting order

In general terms, the batting line-up usually follows the following format:

• *lead-off* – the first batter should have a high on-base average, possess a good eye, not swing at bad pitches and be a good baserunner
• *second* – should have good bat control, so that he can bunt or hit-and-run if required (see pp. 30–1). Ideally this batter should be left-handed so that he can put the ball between first and second bases, and he should also possess good speed
• *third* – the best batter on the team
• *fourth, fifth, sixth* – big power hitters, to drive round any runners on base

29

- *seventh, eighth and ninth* – generally the weakest hitters in the line-up.

## Switch hitters

Batters are usually either right- or left-handed, but a 'switch' hitter can hit from either side of the plate. This may give him an advantage over the pitcher, batting right-handed against left-handed pitchers and vice-versa.

## The bunt

This is a tactical move used when a batter has less than two strikes against him. (If he bunts foul on the third strike, he is out.) By moving one hand up the bat, the batter cushions the impact and deadens the ball, creating a soft hit to the infield or down the lines. This should not only surprise the fielding team, but should also cause fielding problems: depending on its location, the bunt should draw either the first or third baseman of his base.

The main purpose off a bunt is to advance players into a scoring position – although if the batter is fast enough, he could bunt for a base hit. If there is a runner on first base and a weak hitter at the plate, a successful bunt will advance the runner to second base. From second, the runner should score on any subsequent base hit. This strategy will normally only be used when there are less than two outs.

Bunting requires a great deal of skill and self-confidence. The bunt must be good – i.e. on the ground near the base lines – and runners should not break for the next base until the ball hits the ground.

## The 'suicide squeeze' or 'squeeze play'

This is when a batter deliberately sacrifices himself in order for a baserunner to score. It normally occurs with a runner on third base, usually with fewer than two outs and late in a close game.

When the pitcher begins his delivery, the runner should be ready to break for home. As the runner is committed to going, the batter must make contact with the ball, even if he can only foul it off. (If the batter fails to connect, the runner will be stranded between the bases.) If the ball is bunted on to the ground in fair territory, the runner will cross home plate before the defence can make a play, although the batter will probably be put out at first. However, if the ball is bunted up into the air, the defence can make an easy double play.

## Sacrifice fly

This is another sacrifice situation used to advance baserunners or allow them to score. For example, with a runner on third base and less than two outs, the batter will deliberately hit a fly ball deep into the outfield so that, even if it is caught, the runner has time to tag up and run safely to home plate.

## Stealing

Base stealing is when a runner breaks for the next base (usually on the pitch) and gets there before the catcher can throw him out. It is therefore a way of advancing around the bases, although should only be undertaken on the instructions of the coaches and by fast runners.

## Stealing second base

This can occur at any time in the game when a fast runner is at first. The ideal pitch to steal on is a breaking ball – e.g. a curveball (*see* p. 20) – since this gives the runner more time to get to second. By stealing second base, the runner should now score on any subsequent base hit.

## Hit-and-run

With a runner on first base and the pitcher behind in the count (i.e. he has thrown more balls than strikes), the 'hit-and-run' is a very effective play for advancing runners.

## Substitution

The manager of the offensive team may change the player at bat for a substitute hitter when a hit is badly needed – e.g. when the bases are loaded. The substitute is known as a 'pinch hitter', and the original batter is then out of the remaining part of the game. The manager may similarly bring on a 'pinch runner' if a given offensive play

---

### Example of a hit-and-run

As the pitcher motions towards the plate (in these situations a fastball is likely, since it is a good pitch to control and it is likely to be a strike), the runner takes off towards second. The batter's job is to protect the runner by hitting a ground ball.

As the runner breaks towards second (*see* fig. 10), hopefully the second baseman will also break to cover the steal. This will leave a gap through which the batter can hit the ball. If the batter hits the gap, the runner should make third base and the hitter should get to first. However, to avoid a double play, it is vital that the ball be hit on the ground *behind* the runner.

---

requires extra speed around the bases. In both instances these substitutes take up the approriate positions in the line-up until more changes are made.

In some leagues a 'designated hitter' is allowed. He bats in place of the pitcher throughout the game if the pitcher is a weak hitter.

---

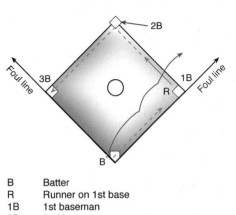

| B | Batter |
|----|--------|
| R | Runner on 1st base |
| 1B | 1st baseman |
| 2B | 2nd baseman |
| 3B | 3rd baseman |
| ⟶ | Path of runner breaking to steal 2nd base |
| ⟶ | 2nd baseman covering steal on 2nd base |
| ⟶ | Ground hit to right field behind runner |
| - - -> | Path of runner to 2nd and 3rd bases, and batter to first |

▲ *Fig. 10 Example of a hit-and-run*

# Coaching positions

## Manager

The manager usually watches the game from the bench. He is in charge of the team's overall strategy, sending signals to the base coaches that will determine what plays he wants the team to make.

## Base coaches

The base coaches are on the offensive (batting) side and stand in the coaching boxes at first and third bases. Their primary role is to direct the baserunners, telling them when to:

- hold up (i.e. at second or third base)
- advance to the next base
- 'slide' (*see* p. 24)
- steal (*see* p. 30)

as well as the location of the ball, and so on. The third base coach also calls the offensive plays, using a series of signals that the team has devised.

# The umpires

The most difficult, yet possibly the most rewarding role in baseball is that of the umpire. As a sport, baseball has many little technicalities and nuances, which make it both fascinating and frustrating at the same time. The majority of decisions are based on the umpire's split-second judgement (e.g. whether or not a fastball is in the strike zone), and to this end he is always liable to be second-guessed by players and coaches alike. While baseball allows managers and coaches to appeal against an umpire's decision on technical aspects (such as the rules and their interpretation), they cannot appeal against judgement decisions.

In most amateur games, umpires work in pairs, operating a two-man system. In this system there is a 'home-plate' umpire and a 'base' umpire. The plate umpire is positioned directly behind the catcher, and therefore needs to wear specialised protective equipment.

## Clothing and equipment

The umpire's uniform consists of grey trousers, a pale blue shirt, an umpire's cap and black shoes – with metal toe plates for protection against foul balls. The plate umpire also has a small black ball bag attached to his belt. It should be large enough to hold three baseballs.

### Protection

Most umpires today use 'inside protectors' that are worn under the shirt to protect the chest, shoulders and upper arms, and leg guards to provide protection for the insteps, ankles, shins and knees. A standard umpire's mask is obviously vital for protection of the throat area and the side of the head. Most are lightweight and are therefore comfortable to use throughout the whole game. It is vital that the mask allows excellent visibility.

## Indicator

The indicator is a small, hand-held device that the umpire uses to keep track of the 'count' – i.e. balls, strikes and the number of outs (*see* p. 14).

## Plate brush

The plate brush is used to clear the home plate of dirt and any other debris. It is vital that the pitcher, batter and umpire should be able to see the plate clearly at all times.

# Responsibilities

## Plate umpire

The primary responsibility of the plate umpire is to call balls and strikes, although he also judges whether a runner reaches home plate (and hence scores a run) without being tagged, and calls 'time-out' if requested by a player (e.g. in the case of injury).

## Base umpire

In the two-man system, the base umpire has a lot of ground to cover. His job is to make the call at the respective bases (i.e. decide whether the runner is safe or out).

## Before the game

Before entering the field, both umpires must have a thorough understanding of their own – and their fellow umpire's – duties and responsibilities, especially since sometimes there are several possible plays at different bases. It is vital that both umpires agree whose base it is, and who is to make the call. They should also ensure that any rule interpretations are clarified beforehand.

Upon arrival at the field the umpires need to check the field of play, ensuring that it is safe to play on and conforms to league requirements. The lines must be marked correctly and the bases, home plate and pitching rubber must be in the correct position and secure.

## Starting the game

Once the line-up cards have been handed to the plate umpire, the game has started. At this point the umpires, together with the two managers, should discuss the ground rules. These are any rules that are peculiar to that field of play.

Once the pitcher has completed his warm-up pitches, the lead-off batter is called to the plate, the plate umpire shouts, 'Play ball!', and the game can begin.

## After the game

Immediately following the game, the umpires should leave the field together. They should complete any necessary reports, and forward them to the appropriate officials.

# Umpires' signals

Although the rules of baseball do not have a standardised set of umpires' signals, the following are almost universally recognised.

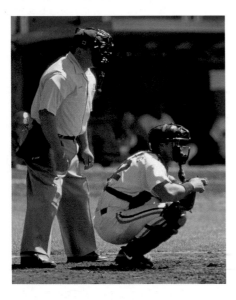

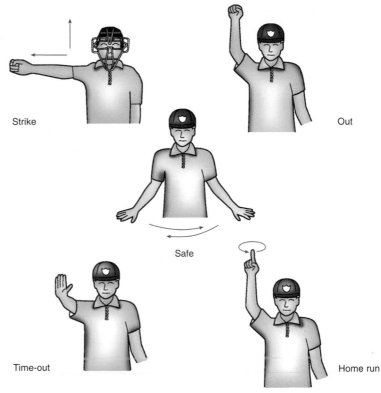

Strike

Out

Safe

Time-out

Home run

▲ *Fig. 11  Universally recognised umpires' signals*

# The scorer

Scorers are necessary at all official baseball games. It is their job to score the game accurately, compile the official scorecard, and send the relevant statistics to the respective league officials. Batting averages and all other averages are compiled by league officials after the game, once everything has been confirmed.

Statistics play an important part in baseball, past and present, with official records on elements like hits, outs, base hits, steals, errors and catches for various games dating back more than 100 years. Accurate scoring is therefore vital to keep track of these records; it goes far beyond merely keeping score of the game, and it is the scorer's responsibility to make judgements on whether or not a fielder should be credited with an error etc.

## The scorecard

The scorecard is made up of four main parts.

### Batting linc-up

In this section the scorer lists each player's name and fielding position, in the order in which they are to bat. There are spaces in which the introduction of any substitutes into the game may be noted.

### Game record

This essentially records the game as it progresses. For every batter there is a box, in which the scorer marks the player's progress as they advance from base to base around the diamond.

The game record also has a section for recording balls and strikes. This is important and can act as a double-check if there are any queries regarding the umpire's count.

Finally, the scorer will use this section to keep a running record – for each inning – of runs scored, the number of safe hits, errors by the fielding team, and the number of runners left on base.

### Box score

This is where the scorer lists all the relevant statistics for each team's batting and fielding performance. These can be a valuable resource for coaches and fans alike.

### Pitching statistics

This records the details of the pitching performance, listing a wide variety of statistical information.

### Other sections

As well as the four main parts described above, the scorecard also includes a section for catchers, which notes their name and how many 'passed balls' they allowed. A passed ball is when the catcher fails to stop a pitch that should have been stopped with normal effort, allowing a base runner to advance.

Finally there is a section which lists 'double' and 'triple plays' (see p. 29), noting all of the players involved.

# Softball

## Fundamentals of the game

The game of softball was derived from baseball, and there are many similarities between them.

Two teams take it in turn to bat and field, with a pitcher delivering the ball to the batter, who attempts to hit it and run around as many bases on the softball diamond as possible before the ball is fielded and brought back to the infield by the defensive team. As with baseball, the batter/runner can either stop at any or all of the three bases *en route*, or can run around in one go if he hits a home run.

The defensive team attempts to get the batters and baserunners out in the same ways as in baseball (*see* pp. 14–15), and once three players on the offensive team are out, the two teams switch. There are seven innings in softball (rather than nine), and an inning is completed when each team has batted.

Softball in the UK is essentially an amateur sport, with many games being played for fun both inside and outside of official league structures. But softball is also played competitively in national and international tournament and championship competitions. The following pages detail the main *differences* between the games of softball (both fast- and slow-pitch) and baseball, so it is worth reading pp. 10–16 to get a general overview of the game and their similarities first.

# The playing area

Softballs are bigger and heavier than baseballs (*see* p. 40), so they travel more slowly through the air and cannot be thrown or hit as far. Softball diamonds are therefore smaller than their baseball counterparts, although the exact measurements depend on whether 'fast-' or 'slow-pitch' softball is being played (see pp. 42–3), and whether it is a male, female, mixed or youth game. The batting box, pitcher's circle and catcher's area are also smaller than in baseball, and there is no pitcher's mound in softball.

Figure 12 illustrates the softball field, with the various dimensions noted on p. 39.

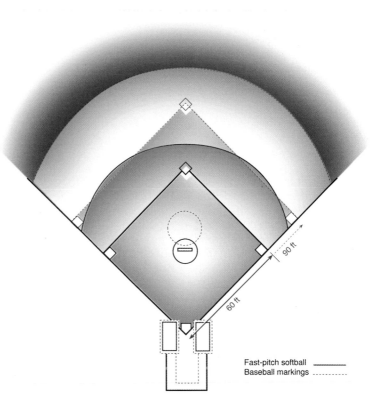

Fast-pitch softball ———
Baseball markings ··········

▲  *Fig. 12   The fast-pitch softball pitch compared with the baseball pitch*

# Softball pitch dimensions

## Fast-pitch

|  | Distance between bases | Distance from pitcher's plate to home plate |
|---|---|---|
| Male | 60 ft (18.29 m) | 46 ft (14.02 m) |
| Female | 60 ft (18.29 m) | 40 ft (12.19 m) |

## Slow-pitch

|  |  | Distance between bases | Distance from pitcher's plate to home plate |
|---|---|---|---|
| Male |  | 65 ft (19.18 m) | 50 ft (15.24 m) |
| Female |  | 65 ft (19.18 m) | 50 ft (15.24 m) |
| Mixed |  | 65 ft (19.18 m) | 50 ft (15.24 m) |
| Youth |  |  |  |
|  | U-10 | 55 ft (16.76 m) | 35 ft (10.67 m) |
|  | U-12 | 60 ft (18.29 m) | 40 ft (12.19 m) |
|  | U-14 | 65 ft (19.18 m) | 46 ft (14.02 m) |
|  | 14+ | 65 ft (19.81 m) | 50 ft (15.24 m) |

# Equipment

Most softball equipment is the same as in baseball (*see* pp. 7–9), with the following exceptions.

## The ball

Although they are manufactured in the same way, softballs are larger and heavier than baseballs, with a circumference of between 11⅞ and 12⅛ in. (29.9–31 cm) and weight of 6¼–7 oz (177–189 g).

## The bat

The softball bat is shorter, thinner and heavier than the baseball bat:

• maximum length: 34 in. (86.4 cm)
• maximum diameter at its thickest part: 2¼ in. (5.7 cm)
• maximum weight: 38 oz (1.1 kg)
but like a baseball bat can be made of either wood or aluminium.

## Gloves

These are larger than baseball gloves to allow for the larger ball.

# Playing positions

The playing positions in fast-pitch soft-ball (*see* p. 42) are the same as in base-ball. However, there are ten players in the slow-pitch game (*see* pp. 42–3), an additional outfielder – called the 'rover' – sharing responsibility for the centre field (*see* fig. 13). He tends to play to the right of the centre field area, with the centre fielder playing further over to the left.

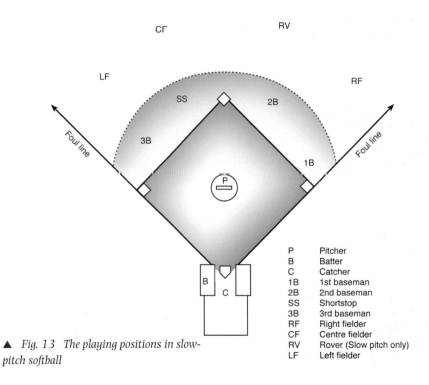

| | |
|---|---|
| P | Pitcher |
| B | Batter |
| C | Catcher |
| 1B | 1st baseman |
| 2B | 2nd baseman |
| SS | Shortstop |
| 3B | 3rd baseman |
| RF | Right fielder |
| CF | Centre fielder |
| RV | Rover (Slow pitch only) |
| LF | Left fielder |

▲  *Fig. 13  The playing positions in slow-pitch softball*

# Different versions of softball

There are two basic types of softball, 'fast-pitch' and 'slow-pitch', defined mainly by the speed at which the ball is pitched to the batter.

## Fast-pitch softball

Fast-pitch softball is the international competition form of the game, and Women's Fast-pitch is an Olympic Medal Sport. It is usually played in the UK as a single-sex sport.

It is essentially an underarm version of baseball: all other aspects of the game, including the techniques, are the same with the exception of the pitching technique.

### Pitching technique

The pitcher stands with both feet in contact with the pitching plate, with one shoulder pointing to first base and the other to third. Before delivering the ball, the pitcher holds it with both hands in front of his body for not less than one second but not more than ten. The ball must remain in view of the batter once one hand has been removed and the pitch commences.

The pitcher is allowed to take one step towards the batter when delivering the ball, and uses an underarm 'windmill' pitching action. One revolution of the arm is allowed, which imparts speed, together with a whipping action from the wrist. The ball is released below the hip, and the wrist should be no further from the body than the elbow.

### Strike zone

The strike zone is slightly larger than in baseball (see fig. 14), stretching from the knees to the armpits in a normal batting position (the batter cannot crouch down to make the target smaller).

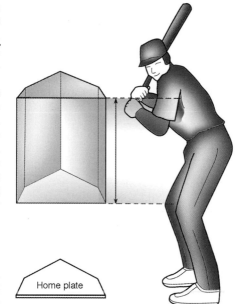

▲ *Fig. 14  The strike zone in fast-pitch softball*

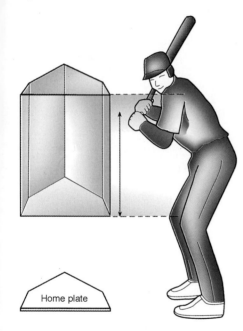

▼ *Fig. 15   The strike zone in slow-pitch softball*

Home plate

# Slow-pitch softball

Slow-pitch softball accounts for 95% of softball played in the UK. Most teams are mixed, with men and women batting alternately.

Whereas baseball and softball are games dominated by pitching, slow-pitch softball is essentially a hitting and fielding game. Apart from the additional tenth player, the main differences between slow-pitch and baseball/fast-pitch softball are:

• stealing from one base to another is not allowed (*see* p. 30): a runner cannot leave his base until the ball passes over home plate
• the strike zone is more generous (*see* fig. 15): this stretches from the batter's knees to the back shoulder as he stands at home plate in a normal batting position
• pitching style
• a ball hit foul after two strikes results in a strike-out.

## Pitching technique

The pitcher must start with either one or both feet in contact with the pitching plate. He can take one step in any direction, but one foot must remain in contact with the plate until the ball is released.

The ball must be delivered in an underarm arc which is 6–12 ft (1.83–3.66 m) off the ground at the top of its trajectory (*see* fig. 16, p. 44). Anything else will be deemed illegal and count as a ball (unless the batter swings at it). The pitch must also be thrown at a moderate speed, or the pitcher risks dismissal from the match.

To compensate for lack of speed, the pitcher therefore employs a combination of different spins, speeds and arc height. This makes the delivery as awkward as possible for the batter, and also forces him to hit the ball in a certain way – ideally ground balls and fly balls, allowing the fielding side the opportunity to make appropriate defensive plays.

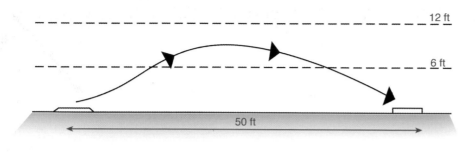

▲ *Fig. 17  Pitching trajectory in slow-pitch softball*

# Youth programmes

Baseball/Softball UK operate youth programmes aimed at developing baseball and softball, and these include schools programmes, community leagues, youth leagues and camps for youngsters to attend.

There are also three main development programmes:

- 'Modified Schools Softball', aimed at 10–16-year-olds
- 'Pitch Hit and Run', aimed at primary schools
- 'PlayBall!', aimed at 9–12-year-olds in local communities

the latter two being run in conjunction with Major League Baseball.

**Baseball/Softball UK**

Ariel House
74 A Charlotte Street
London W1P 1LR
Tel: 020 7453 7055
Fax: 020 7453 7007
www.baseballsoftballuk.com

**Major League Baseball**

Ariel House
74A Charlotte Street
London W1P 1LR
Tel: 020 7453 7000
Fax: 020 7453 7007
www.majorleaguebaseball.com

# Glossary

**Balk** – an illegal action by the pitcher with a runner on base, resulting in all runners advancing one base

**Ball** – a pitch that does not enter the strike zone, and is not swung at by the batter

**Base** – situated at each corner of the infield diamond

**Baserunner** – *see* 'runner'

**Base on balls** – the batter is awarded first base by the umpire if the pitcher throws four pitches outside the strike zone, at which the batter does not swing (also called a 'walk')

**Bases loaded** – when runners are on first, second and third bases

**Batting order** – the order in which batters go up to bat

**Batter's box** – the area in which the batter must stand when batting

**Bench** – the area of the field where the teams sit: also called the 'dugout'

**Bottom** – the second half of any inning

**Breaking ball** – any baseball pitch that deviates in flight, e.g. curveball, slider, knuckleball

**Bunt** – when the batter allows the ball to hit the bat, creating a soft hit to the infield

**Catch** – where the fielder catches the ball in the air, without it touching the ground

**Catcher** – the player who fields directly behind the batter

**Catcher's box** – the area in which the catcher must stay until the pitcher delivers the ball

**Catcher's interference** – where the catcher impedes the batter, for which the batter is awarded first base

**Change-up** – a slow baseball pitch, usually thrown with the same motion as a fastball, thereby deceiving the batter

**Count** – the number of balls and strikes against the batter

**Curveball** – a baseball pitch that curves in flight

**Cut-off** – a player who receives a throw from the outfield

**Dead ball** – when the ball is out of play

**Double** – a two-base hit

**Double play** – when the fielding team gets two offensive players out on one continuous play

**Error** – a fielding mistake, especially one that would have put a runner out

**Fair ball** – a ball hit into fair territory

**Fair territory** – the area of the field between first and third baselines

**Fastball** – a baseball pitch thrown as fast as possible

**Fast-pitch softball** – an underarm version of baseball

**Fly ball** – a ball that is hit into the air

**Force play** – when a baserunner is forced to advance to the next base by the runner behind

**Foul ball** – a ball that does not go into fair territory

**Foul territory** – that part of the field lying outside the first and third base-lines

**Foul tip** – a batted ball which goes sharply backwards

**Ground ball** – a hit that bounces or rolls on the ground

**Ground rules** – rules which make allowances for any field obstructions

**Hit** – when a batter reaches base after hitting successfully

**Home run** – scored when a hit allows a batter to run around all the bases and back to home plate in one go without stopping

**Infield fly** – a hit into the air in the infield, which the fielders do not have to catch to obtain an out

**Infielder** – a player who plays in the infield

**Inning** – when both teams have batted once, an inning is complete

**Knuckleball** – a speciality baseball pitch that deviates in flight

**Middle infielders** – the collective name for the second baseman and shortstop

**Out** – when the batting team have a player out (three outs per inning)

**Pitch** – a ball delivered by the pitcher to the batter

**Pitch out** – a pitch deliberately thrown wide of the plate, to help the catcher throw out base stealers

**Pop fly** – a ball that is hit high into the air

**Relief pitcher** – a substitute pitcher

**Rover** – the additional outfielder in slow-pitch softball

**Run** – scored when a runner touches all the bases in the correct order and returns to home plate

**Run down** – when a runner is caught between bases

**Runner** – an offensive player who is on or running towards any base

**Screwball** – a speciality baseball pitch

**Single** – a one-base hit

**Slide** – an offensive move along the ground to reach base

**Slider** – a baseball pitch that breaks at the last minute

**Slow-pitch softball** – softball format where the emphasis is on batting rather than pitching

**Split-fingered fastball** – a fastball that dips at the last minute: also called a 'forkball'

**Steal** – when a runner attempts to reach the next base before the base-man tags him out (not allowed in slow-pitch softball)

**Strike** – a legal pitch if: i) the batter swings and misses; ii) the ball passes through the strike zone; iii) the ball is hit into foul territory (on the first two strikes only); iv) the batter swings at the ball and the ball hits him whilst in the strike zone

**Strike-out** – when a batter is called out on strikes

**Strike zone** – the area over home plate through which a pitch must pass to be called a 'strike', and individual to each batter

**Tag** – when a player touches the runner with the ball to obtain an out

**Top** – the first half of any inning

**Triple** – a three-base hit

**Triple play** – when the fielding team gets three players out at once (hence ending the inning in one play)

**Walk** – *see* base on balls

# Index